Getting Ready for
COLLEGE
Jump to It!!!

Getting Ready for COLLEGE

Jump to It!!!

DR. MABLE SCOTT

authorHOUSE®

AuthorHouse™ LLC
1663 Liberty Drive
Bloomington, IN 47403
www.authorhouse.com
Phone: 1-800-839-8640

Published by AuthorHouse   11/14/2013

ISBN: 978-1-4918-1073-6 (sc)
ISBN: 978-1-4918-1071-2 (hc)
ISBN: 978-1-4918-1072-9 (e)

Library of Congress Control Number: 2013915499

CONTENTS

ACKNOWLEDGEMENTS

I would like to thank all of my students who felt the need to share with the audience for whom this book was written. Even though the contribution was worth points towards the semester grade, I appreciate your willingness to contribute your thoughts. I thank all of my friends who encouraged me to continue my quest to help students to become successful. My son, his friend and my granddaughter have been very patient when I went into seclusion and could not come around for family activities. Thank you for your patience. I thank God for the opportunity to share a little of me in this book with my young audience in preparation for a higher education. Lastly, I thank those persons who read my memoirs and gave me feedback to ensure this book held information that students in high school could use to make a decision about going to college.

DEDICATION

This book is dedicated to Chloe Alexis Scott, my three-year-old granddaughter with hopes that she will read this book when she becomes an eighth grader and use it as a tool to prepare her for college. I also dedicate this book to the scholarship ministry of my church who help children with preparation for a higher education.

About the Author

Dr. Mable Scott is currently a fifth year associate professor of physical education at South Carolina State University. Dr. Scott is co-sponsor of the Health and Physical Education club where she is encouraging and training students to become effective physical education teachers. She coerces students to nurture communication and physical skills.

Dr. Scott taught all grade levels in public school over a period of twenty-six years and was a successful school administrator for seven years. Much of Dr. Scott's educational experience has been working with at-risk students. She has and continues to encourage them to make decisions that lead to successful, healthy living and with helping them to believe in themselves. She has inspired many children to go on to college to pursue a career that serves others.

INTRODUCTION

Working with college students has inspired me to write a guide that will help motivate and prepare 9th graders for college. The first thing any student should know is that anyone can go to college, but should not be pushed into college. That is an individual decision. College is an institution of higher learning. If you are prepared to go to college, meaning, there is a desire to go, the next step is to make sure the person has the academic tools to succeed upon arriving. "For students to be truly ready for college, they need to demonstrate that they can apply the knowledge they have learned in their academic courses through performances that exhibit the foundational skills of the academic discipline—for example, expository writing, literary, historical and scientific analysis and research papers" Lenz (2007). I have been an associate professor at SC State University for five Years, and I have noticed that a great many of my students are not academically prepared to complete the class assignments which eventually put a damper on them competing for jobs if they graduate.

Students are challenged with several mediocre, not rigorous, assignments that it doesn't take a rocket scientist to tackle. However, because some students are admitted to college without the necessary academic background, many are not successful. What do I mean by successful? Students who are not academically prepared for higher level thinking or higher level assignments are not experiencing success. I find it hard to believe that college level students do not know how to study. "No matter how successful a student you were, experience has shown that the learning skills you employed in high school will likely not be sufficient to guarantee success in your college courses" (Leigher, 2000). In addition to studying, there are other issues that pose as hindrances to students' academic success. Reading is an issue. Writing is an even bigger issue. Attending class is an issue. Participating in extracurricular activities is an issue. Supporting school-sponsored activities is an issue. Why are these young people in college? I can't answer that! What I can tell you is those students who come to college academically ready are the students who succeed. They are the students who do not let relationships get in the way of their studies, and they are careful to choose the nonacademic activities that will not get in the way of their successes.

Over the past few semesters, I have asked my students to share with me what they would do differently to prepare for college if they could go back to high school and start again. In most high schools, the grade level starts at 9th grade; thus, this book was designed for 9th-12th graders. In my classes, I teach mostly sophomores and juniors, that is second and third year students. I asked my students to concentrate on three areas: academics, extra-curricular activities and relationships. By the second year of college, students are able to analyze the challenges of high school versus challenges in college.

I was amazed at the responses and thought they were worth sharing; thus, the heart of this book. I sincerely believe that the comments that I am about to share will help you and other young people like you to better prepare for college. If you are seriously thinking about going to college, these thoughts will give any student reasons to pull their act together and do whatever is necessary to make plans for attending college. Students should also take something to college with them that will enable them to become successful, productive people while in college and once the academic challenge is finished. Each and every student who desires to attend college should be well equipped with skills that include: time management, test taking, reading, note taking, and interacting with others. Select the college or university of your choice or at least a college or university that is affordable.

Preparing for the college adventure really starts when one is in primary school, but who thinks about higher education then. Waiting until 9th grade is possibly the last chance you will get to pull your act together well enough to be successful once you get to college. From the strongest assessments of students that I have served, I found they did not fail because they wanted to fail; they failed because they did not possess the necessary academic skills needed for their success.

Consequently, some students are intrinsically motivated and are able to overcome their academic shortcomings. Students in the 9th grade are old enough to understand that study habits play an important part in academic success. If you have not developed any study habits by 9th grade, you still have time to grow a set of "good study habits." If you feel lost in academics by 9th grade, you still have time to get some tutoring, so the direction of your academics has a path in which to move. Once you get to 9th grade, you receive credits for the classes you take. This is the beginning of the track for a grade point average (GPA), and every class you take from this point on, you will receive credits that comprise a grade point average that will be viewed for several reasons. Reasons include high school class ranking, college admission, pledging, scholarships, and maybe even job hiring.

This book is an appeal to all 8th and 9th graders. Please get your act together and put your head deep down in your books. All of you have an opportunity to earn a scholarship of some kind to pay college expenses. Each of you now has the same opportunities to be successful by giving teachers your undivided attention. Understand what goes on in the learning process and become a part of that process. Pay attention to how you learn and seek help if you need assistance in organizing your thoughts. Ask your teacher a lot of questions or search for answers to your questions over the internet. You will be practicing your research and reading skills. As a 9th grader, you should consider one or more careers and learn about what it takes to get there. Make plans now and follow your plans. By high school graduation, it would be beneficial to you if you know your career path and if you have chosen a college based on that career. College needs you just as much as you need college.

CHAPTER 1

FOCUS ON YOURSELF

In case no one ever told you, allow me to tell you that you are the most important person in your life. You can be as selfish or as generous as you like. By now, you have made that decision as to what kind of person you are going to be. You have been working on the person inside of you since as far back as second grade, maybe even first grade or kindergarten. You will be who you are, maybe for the rest of your life, unless God sees fit to stir you in another direction. Meaning, if you made a decision to not be a giving person, God could step in and keep someone from giving you something that you really need to save your life; such as a kidney or heart. Maybe God will step in and do just the opposite and allow someone to donate a vital organ to change your perspective about being a giving person if someone saves your life. Here is another scenario. Let's just suppose that you made a decision to do criminal acts, and you are out there with your friends knocking over mailboxes or robbing stores or breaking in cars just for the fun of it. God may provide a reason to stop you by allowing you to get caught or injured during one of your episodes.

At any rate, we are not going to decide to become a criminal. I believe students turn to criminal acts just to see how smart they can be, but believe me, you are not going to out-smart technology. If you look at CSI, Crime Scene Investigation or Forensic Files, then those stories tell how investigators caught the criminal and should let you know that the common thinking brain is going to get caught. I decided as a first grader when I was sent to the office for the first time that I would not get in trouble at school or anywhere else. The grass at school had not been cut in a while, so the grass was growing what we call onions tops. My friends and I developed a way to shoot those onion tops at each other.

1

Our teacher, Mrs. Gold, sent six of her students to the office. Our 6'5" principal stood hovering over us, and I was scared out of my mind because I heard my mother tell Mr. Pendergrass what to do to my brother, "Don't call me; you spank his behind when he cuts up at school, and I will spank his behind when he cuts up at home." Well, I knew he knew we were sister and brother, and the message would be the same or worse for me if he called my house. When he took out his strap, I started crying so loud that he just threatened to use it, scolded us and sent us back to class. From then on my motto was "I am not doing anything that I think my parents would cut my behind about or that would land me in trouble with the authorities." I STILL LIVE BY THAT TODAY.

I want you to concentrate on the positives in your life. Remember, "The first law of nature is self-preservation. Cut off that which may harm you. But if it is worth preserving, and is meaningful, nourish it and have no regrets. Ultimately, this is true living and love of self . . . from within" (Hodge, 2009).

Right now, you are a positive force in your life. In most school districts, discipline records are expunged, unless there has been some criminal issue that everyone who teaches you should know about. The mere fact that you are reading this book tells me that you do not have a record of violence following you. Entering 9th grade tells everyone that you must be doing some academic work in school to get this far. I can also conclude that you are involved in some type of extracurricular activity either at school or in the community. I strongly believe that you have a great support system of family, friends and it may even extend as wide as church members, peers and organization affiliates. Let your supporters play out their role in your life, and you do your part. Your family consists of your mother, father, sisters, brothers, grandparents, Godparents, uncles, aunts, cousins and whoever else claims you as family. Family will encourage you and cheer for you when you do good things at school, at home or in the community. They want you to be successful, but be careful that other youth might be envious of your success. Sometimes they might not make good decisions or intentionally stir you in the wrong direction out of spite or jealousy.

Watch what they do and how they behave before you make a decision to listen to other youth, including siblings and cousins. They are probably around your age and may not have experienced a lot to advise you and your peers. Get to know them before taking their advice on a serious issue.

Let's go back to making a decision of being selfish or generous. There is nothing wrong with being selfish. Let me explain what that means before you go to bobbing your head in agreement. I believe that a person should look great because it makes you feel great, but do not turn your nose up at the person who cannot afford to dress like you. I always thought that those persons who looked great being dressed up every day were a little arrogant, self-centered, cantankerous-acting people, and people like me who did not have very much found other ways to feel great like athletics and academics. In another book, I will share my story, but for now, let's concentrate on you.

Always remember that how you feel about yourself will impact what you do with your life, what you allow others to do to you and who you will become as a result. If you believe you can, then you can. If you believe you can't, then you can't. You must believe that you are the most important force in your life, and you should decide now which direction you want to travel for the rest of your life. Persons who are generous receive Grace from God. The generosity in a person allows them to give of themselves, and they are willing to love and help a fellowman. Generous persons put the well-being of others first, and that's not to neglect self, but to give of yourself. You can offer to help a peer learn a concept in math or a skill in physical education or assist with a science lab assignment. I never had any money, but I sure helped a lot of people at school. My friends couldn't have my homework, but I showed them how to do the assignment. When I was in class, as soon as I learned a new concept in Algebra, I wanted to help others understand, because my 9th grade math teacher was a little over our heads as most math teachers. I live by the Golden Rule that I learned in Sunday School and Vacation Bible School "Do unto others as you would have them do unto you." Luke 6:31 (Holy Bible)

Another important fact to remember is to learn to dress for the occasion. Even if you do not have a lot of fashionable clothes, you still need to be appropriately dressed for the occasion at hand. School is a place to wear casual clothes, but there are some who wear party or beach wear to school. If your everyday look is a dressed-up one, when there is a time to dress up, you will not appear to have done anything to give yourself an exclusive look. If your choice of a blouse is low cut, tank, see-through or tie-back like beach wear, then when you go to the beach party, what will people see that is new. They would have seen your body long before you get to the beach party.

Using cell phones in class can be a distraction and a very awful habit to take to school. It is very rude of any student to sit in class on the telephone or text friends when your teacher is present and in the middle of a lesson. You can use your cell phone in class to search answers to questions from your teacher, but let your teacher know what you are doing. Otherwise, use the cell phone before or after class/school, during lunch, during the change of classes or even during a restroom break. Do not allow the phone to distract you from getting your assignments done in class because you are waiting for a phone call, texting inside of your book bag or you are leaving class to talk on the phone.

I represent all teachers when I say that we have very little patience with students who try to sneak and use their phone during class, then get upset when reprimanded about it. Most of my students tell me they are speaking to their mom which I do not believe. Unless it is something urgent, mom and dad should know when you have class and when you are free if they are going to call you during the school day. Your friends should know as well. It is up to you to inform family and friends when to and when not to call you.

Keep in mind that you should always demonstrate respect for yourself and others in everything you do. Respect your teachers. Respect your family who will be around to support you when everyone else might give up on you or desert you. Respect your teachers who work hard to ensure learning takes place. Respect your peers who need to be shown love and a sense of acceptance from you and others. Respect yourself by following rules and procedures and most of all completing all assignments on time.

The last thing that I am going to focus on in this chapter is the fact that you should not be overly concerned about how other people perceive you. Over the years, I learned people are going to talk about you whether you do something good or bad or nothing at all. Make it your business to give them a better perspective of you. Be selective of the friends you hang with and make it your business to get grades that will enable you to qualify for various scholarships offered by your state. Grades represent the diligence of your work ethic in all subjects. Colleges and universities look at grades like you look at the amount of money you make on a job. You really want to make the highest grades you can while in high school.

CHAPTER 2

PHYSICAL ACTIVITY FOR LIFE

The very first thing the doctor may recommend after surgery is a short walk around the halls depending on the type of surgery. Your surgeon or therapist may recommend that you exercise from 10 to 15 minutes 3 to 5 times a day during the early recovery period. As the short walks lengthen, so does strength and endurance. The doctor knows that physical activity has lots of benefits that aid any medicine the patient could be given. Some doctors use exercise as a natural prescription to wellness. Exercising will also help you feel better, have more energy and perhaps even live longer. Exercising can be fun, promote better sleep, combat health conditions, control weight, and improve moods.

Physical education teachers encourage and provide lots of reasons why the body should stay active. Students are taught that physical activity increases oxygen intake which leads to a stronger heart, mind and soul. The curriculum in every school district requires students to get credits in physical education or some equivalent course such as dance, ROTC, or band that offers physical activity.

The benefits of being physically active are aligned with a person's level of fitness. There are all sorts of benefits to being physically active to include: health benefits, cognitive benefits, social benefits and emotional benefits. As a person engages in physical activity, the benefits might be implemented, enhanced, or maintained. These benefits improve a person's long term and short term health and well-being. If one type of benefit is unbalanced, the entire body is off balance. When one's health is at its best, work is easier.

Being physically active yields well-developed muscles, bones and joints and improves muscular strength, muscular flexibility, balance, agility, and coordination. Healthy children tend to feel confident with participating in physical activities. Children should get outdoors to be physically active through play with friends and neighbors. Research is under way to determine if the technological electronics contribute to the delinquency of children's health or do those same devices positively affect children's fitness levels.

Through play, children can discover their physical capabilities, explore skill levels and unravel the understanding of their cognitive development. Diamond (1998) revealed that "play helps set the stage for higher order brain functions, such as decoding messages and problem solving." Children who are healthy tend to perform better in school and are less prone to injury while at play. Physical activity generates more blood with fresh oxygen to the brain for increased concentration and decreased fatigue which leads to children becoming mentally alert.

The many social benefits from physical activities meet the desire to become accepted by friends and family. Becoming involved in physical activities will almost always lead to involvement with others who are close in age and with equivalent skills. Among the reasons people find ways to get involved in physical activities are those that bring them close to other people or to socialize with others. For instance, boredom, team play, social contact, competition, challenge, meeting new people, interaction with mate, contact with family, and countless other reasons. Physical activity allows for interaction with others to alleviate loneliness and feelings of isolation.

Emotionally, success brings on increased feelings of healthy self-esteem. Physical activity impacts the psychological well-being which expands when children are challenged to learn and/or master new physical skills. When children are faced with new challenges, they are under pressure to succeed. Internal reasons to participate in physical activities include: enjoying nature, escaping from routine, self-improvement, recognition, intellectual stimulation and many other reasons.

All school curriculums should include physical education for all grades. An effective physical education program should provide lots of physical activities and encourage children to participate in activities away from class for a recommended 30-60 minutes daily either indoors or outdoors. It is also recommended that children spend more time actively engaged in physical activities and less time watching non-relevant television shows and playing non-productive video games.

The choice to get involved with physical activities is left up to the individual person. For the person who eats far more calories than are burned off during physical activities will surely store the unused calories and will gain weight. The person who exercises more than the caloric intake will surely lose weight. The person who exercises just enough to burn the calories that are eaten will maintain their weight. Certainly, there are severe consequences to not being physically active. The physically inactive person stands a chance of becoming overweight or obese, developing diabetes or other chronic diseases, having a poor fitness level, acquiring poor health conditions, decreasing mobility, and more.

CHAPTER 3

FOCUS ON ACADEMICS

School should always be challenging. The curriculum should be designed with love and rigor to show anybody reading it that the classroom will be a place where students are challenged; not just a place to do the work, but to do quality work. Students of this 21st century would not have survived the academic challenge from teachers of the 19th or 20th centuries. There is truth in the statement that "you can't make me." Teachers hear that now. As a teacher, I have heard it, but my teachers in the 50's and 60's actually did make you get your work done, and it had to be quality work, or it was not accepted. I did not necessarily admire all of my teachers then, but as I think back, I loved the drive, the coaching and the firmness used by my teachers to help me and my classmates get our work done. They were determined to have students who learned what they were teaching. Our teachers would stop a student at the door and ask that they tuck in shirts, comb hair and come with a book. I had a teacher who would not let you in the door if you did not have paper and pencil. Unfortunately, some students still failed, but the number was far less than what educators face today.

I never was a straight "A" student. I was motivated by those who were "A" students, and I rubbed elbows with them. I wanted to make "A's" like them, but that didn't always happen. My teachers never expected me to go to college, but my mom always said my siblings and I would go. I was not on the college track in high school, just the track to graduate. Most Black schools back in the day, prepared students for college, for technical school or straight for the job market from high school. I guess because I came from a fairly large family and from a low income household, teachers expected me and my siblings to go straight to the job market. But

11

my mind was stuck on hanging on to the coat tail of the straight "A" students, and they were talking about going to college.

I applied and was accepted at South Carolina State College (SCSC) in Orangeburg, South Carolina and Spellman College in Atlanta, Georgia. The gymnastics coaches at the University of South Carolina (USC) asked me about coming there, but they could not find any scholarships to help pay for my education. USC was downtown in the city where I grew up. Spellman had a terrific gymnastics team, but they, too, were not offering any scholarships. Needless to say, I did not know anything about applying for a grant, asking for work study, or getting a loan, so I decided to go to school where I could be away from home and where I could afford to pay out of pocket. I entered the doors of SC State College in the fall of 1970, along with 800 other freshmen. My mom paid for the first semester, and I worked summers and holidays to pay for the other semesters.

I never let anyone to dictate my future, and you must not either. Do not let others define who you are or who you will become. You should decide now while in the 9th grade what career path you would like to pursue and that would put you far ahead in becoming successful. Start working now to be the most highly educated person in your school. Do not think it will be easy, especially if you did not work to your fullest potential during your elementary and middle school days. When you don't apply yourself fully, you might miss some skills and concepts that you will need to be academically successful to leave high school with a fairly decent grade point average (GPA). Put forth every effort to get or polish up those skills because I am certain you will need them when you pursue some form of higher education. What most students do not realize is if you learn the information from teachers the first time around, then the next time you see the same information it should be easier to recall, accept and apply.

I polled several of my college students, so they could share with you their thoughts about getting ready for college. Studies in college are no joke, and in every class that I have taught, I have students who fail my class. Yes, they pay for school! Yet, they still won't get their work done to pass a class. Professors really know how to pour the work on students, and they expect students to have more than a bare minimum amount of knowledge from the class. Almost every student in college would tell you something they should or could have done while in high school to help the transition go much smoother from high school to college.

Freshman female physical education major

"Doing just enough to get by was mainly all I did in high school. I knew it wasn't the right mentality to have, but back then I did not care. I settled for D's and C's and never studied. As long as I passed, I was fine. I did not realize how simple high school was until I finished. If I could go back to high school, I would study everyday and make straight A's."

Junior male activity management major (football player)

"The biggest thing you have to do to prepare for college is take care of business in the classroom. I didn't take my school work very seriously and it put me in a bad situation for college. During my whole high school career I played around and did what I could to get by and on to the next grade. I wish I would have known then in high school what I know now in college, because things would have been much better. I had to bust my tail studying and taking practice tests for the SAT and the ACT, but I made a high enough score to qualify for college."

Sophomore male sports communication major (football player)

"I should have kept my grades up because of scholarships that were offered to me. If my grades were a lot better than they were, I could have gone to the school of my choice. Since I chose to not do my work in class, it really outweighed my options for schools to choose from. Now, I wish that I had listened to what everyone was trying to tell me. If I had to go back to my high school years, I would really focus and put my mind to the test. Playing sports takes some of your time away so that prevented me from studying sometimes, but at the same time I was not trying to study."

Senior female sports communication major

"There are several things that I would do differently during high school to prepare me for college. The main thing I would do is to learn how to study! I NEVER studied in high school because I could get A's and B's without studying, but once I got to college it became a real problem that I did not know HOW I learned and how to EFFECTIVELY study."

Sophomore female nursing major

"My grades in high school reflected the actions of a young person interested in socializing with others and having fun at school. I did not get serious about my grades until my senior year. My grade point average reflected all four years in high school as a whole, regardless of how hard I worked during my senior year. To enter college, your grade point average and entrance exams must both reflect a hard working person who strived for greatness in high school. My test scores were great, but my grade point average could have been better if I had worked harder on it. Working hard at getting good grades in high school would have better prepared me for college."

Senior male physical education major

"The things that I would have done differently in my middle school and high school years that would have helped me transition to college better would be to have tried to form a better relationship with some of my teachers from those years. I didn't really try to do that during those years because I felt like teachers in my school didn't care about their students, seemed like they were just there to collect their checks. That's not true for all of my teachers, but most of them, yes. I think it's good to have teachers that you can relate to. It helps you reinforce the value of education to you as a person and not just another student. Also, I never thought I was incapable or incompetent when it came to my school work, but I was definitely lazy. But I really didn't apply myself to my studies during those years in school. I always did just enough to pass. So I wish I would have applied myself. I believe I could have done a lot better in school."

Freshman male music major

"In my first couple of years of high school my academics were averaging A's and B's. Once I basically knew everyone at my school that became a distraction. I did not pay as much attention to classes as usual. If I could turn back to those days, I would have studied more often. Instead of playing basketball after school or roaming around the community, I should have spent most of that time studying. Reading is another criteria, I only read what needed to be read in high school. Even though, I know "reading is power," I still failed to succeed in college. Most professors expect you to read the material before discussion."

Sophomore female biology major

"My academics were okay in high school. If I could go back, I would prepare myself in high school for college by studying a lot more. I would learn how to stay focused, so I can be rewarded by making good grades in college. I would read more books and participate in more group activities, so I can be prepared for group projects and major assignments. I would also go back and prepare myself by managing on my time for school work, "this way I would not wait until the last minute to do work and be so tired."

Junior "Special Needs" sports communication major

"While in school, I did not start taking it seriously until the end part of my seventh grade year in middle school. I almost failed seventh grade because I did not want to do the work. The reason why I did not do the work was because, I did not understand it, and I was afraid to ask the teacher a question because, I thought the kids would have laughed at me. When my mom found out that I was on the verge of failing, she had a conference with my teacher, and tried to get me some help. During my eighth grade year my parents put me in a private school. I went there my eighth and ninth grade years. When I got back to high school, I had to get used to not having that one on one time with my teachers, but I still did well. The reason for that was because I had a different outlook on school than when I did not know anything. I was not afraid to ask and did not care what people said because, I wanted to go to college and be something in life. I did not get into a serious relationship till the second semester of my senior year."

Freshman female speech major

"The first thing I would change would be my academics. If I had known that my grades played a big part on what college I would attend, I would have made better grades each year in high school and pushed myself to strive to be the best in my class. Also, scholarships would have been helpful because college is so expensive. I should have been on the honor roll during my high school years instead of just during my senior year. I wish that I had taken the ACT earlier than I did instead of waiting till my senior year."

Junior male activity management major

"Some of the things that I would have done differently in high school academically would be that I would have actually paid attention to everything that my teachers and other people told me about getting ready for college. I would have been more focused in on my work and done all my homework on time so that I would be used to doing it in college, because there is no one here in college to tell me or make me do my work. I would have read more so that when I got to college, I would have been used to reading, instead of not wanting to open a book. I would have taken better notes and paid attention in class."

Senior male biology major

"If I had the opportunity to go back to high school and change something before I got to college, I would pay more attention in class. If I had done more I would be going to school for free somewhere on a scholarship. Paying attention in high school would have also helped me to focus and be better prepared for listening in classes because if you missed something, my professor said that there is no guarantee that information will be repeated.

You have read just a few of the comments that my not-so-studious students shared with me. As you read, they have a lot to regret. They learned the hard way that college is no joke. One must bring something to the table to get something out of college, or you will have a miserable time trying to make it and then you fail. In college, professors can tell if you really have mud packs upstairs or a real brain. Now, don't get mud packs mixed up with screw loose or elevator doesn't go to the top or not the sharpest knife in the drawer. Students who have mud packs, really do not and cannot function academically at school as most college students are expected to do. They cannot write. They do not read. They do not participate in class, and most of them very rarely have perfect attendance to class. Let me add to that, those with mud-pack brains are hard to comprehend simple facts. Eventually, the mud-packed brains students do just enough to get by. They easily maintain a 1.65 GPA and are placed on academic probation. Students using their brains usually have a full load of CS (common sense) and they are like sponges who are looking to absorb more knowledge than the professor has prepared to share.

It seems that even academically talented students occasionally allowed distractions to deter them from pursuing six-digit salary careers and admissions into selective and highly selective higher education institutions. As such, being unprepared scholastically, also, influenced the academically talented students' college experiences. Many of them did not produce their greatest output as high school students. As productive college students, however, they now have insight and offer advice. Below, students disclose obstacles regarding academic underachievement that prevented them from seeking admissions into top-ranked universities. Let's read their remarks.

Junior female activity management major

"In high school, I was a student who achieved academic excellence. I graduated in the top 10% of my class and always made the honor roll. I would change my study habits if I could do it all over. I would study and try harder to get a perfect GPA, so that I could've been recognized by other institutions for my academic achievements. Also, I would've taken the SAT and ACT more than twice to improve my score."

Freshman female computer science major

"My grades throughout high school were always very good. I was always in a gifted and talented program, honors, and international baccalaureate program. My mom always wanted me to push myself to greatness. But when I became a senior, I registered for all the easier classes that I needed just to get by. If my mind was on correctly, I would have never done that. I would have taken as many classes as possible, because I basically wasted an opportunity for me to learn something new. I know now that the majority of the things learned in high school, actually do benefit one in college."

Senior female physical education major

"Academically, I was an exemplary student who never missed the principal's honor roll list. I graduated with a 4.2 on a 4.0 scale because I took honors and advanced prep courses because those courses would give more points towards my grade point average. Even through all of the accolades, I felt that throughout my junior and especially senior years, I eased up on my work ethic, and "coasted" to graduation. Sometimes, I sat back and wondered to myself, what would have happened if I put my all into my work. Then instead of just sitting on the stage for graduation, I probably could have been valedictorian."

Senior female special education major

"Academically, I was an average student my freshman and sophomore years. I did my work, but I did not put forth my best effort. Then my junior year I was working really hard because I wanted to go to a good college. I wish I had done terrific starting at the beginning of my freshman year, that way I would not have had to work extra hard my junior year. I should have read over my notes each night, just so I would remember what I had learned that day. I had to learn the hard way because I did not read as often as I should have. Over all, I did well in high school, but I know I could have done better."

Sophomore female business major

"On the academics perspective, I should have been taking academics more seriously. Don't get me wrong, I made the principal's list, as well as had honors classes, but there is always room for improvement. For example, I wish I would have studied more. I would have made better grades, maybe even made the dean's list, but instead I stayed in my comfort zone. If in high school again, I would pay attention to teachers saying "study," then it would not be so hard to study in college."

Academic Tips from College Students

- Learn how to manage your time. School develops the total person academically, socially and emotionally. Have fun, but schedule a time to study every day. Take studying seriously.

- Learn to take notes in class. Note taking is for your own sake. Notes will help you remember what went on in class and the important facts shared by your teacher. Notes give you something to study during your study time.

- Read. Read. Read. Read the required chapters before the next class period to enable you to be actively engaged in the class discussions and to be in the know. Read assigned novels and articles for class. Reading is the key to academic success.

- Studying is a matter of choice. Choose to be prepared.
  Don't wait until the night before an exam or test to cram information into your short term memory. Try daily or weekly reviews to keep you on your toes. The more you familiarize yourself with the information, the easier the test.

- Get enough rest and eat a balanced diet daily. The body recharges itself through sleep. Foods you consume during the day set the mood for the day. Stay away from artificial sugar, soft drinks, caffeine and energy drinks because they tend to make you sluggish and forgetful.

- Work smart. Get outside help if you are struggling in any subject. Waiting until the end of the year or course to try to recover from a low grade is too late. Earn all of the extra credit your instructor offers, but do not depend on extra credit for passing a class. Do what is expected of you and submit assignments on time.

- Reserve time to interact with friends. Surround yourself with positive productive people. Be sure to set aside time for activities that help you relax and relieve the mind and body of stress.

- Narrow your choices for a career/college major by 8th grade, and get more involved with varied courses, school activities, part-time jobs, and people of the community who might be able to help as you enter into college and matriculate through to a degree completion.

- Listen to advice from your parents, grandparents, teachers, counselors, administrators and coaches. Seek help from trustworthy people to make sound, well-thought-out decisions.

- Show your parents that you can make good academic decisions, and they will stay off of your back about studying or working on projects. This is actually a good way to show parents that you are responsible.

- Attend tutoring sessions even though you think you know the subject matter. You just might hear something you missed in class.

- Put all learned information in your long-term memory bank. Once you get to college, you will need that information to help you succeed.

CHAPTER 4

PARTICIPATE IN EXTRACURRICULAR ACTIVITIES

There are several activities, either at school or in the neighborhood, that a student can get involved in while in high school. Activities such as: the school newspaper, band, cheerleading, sports, dance teams, student government, clubs, yearbook publication, community service, chorus, gymnastics, stepping, etc. Getting involved allows students to increase leadership and social skills while affording them with an opportunity to gain knowledge of organizational operations. For instance, students gain insight on budgeting, scheduling, planning, ordering, etc. Another benefit is that students enhance their own sense of belonging which helps them to build self-esteem and character development. Lastly, involvement in extra-curricular activities may possibly influence career choices or offer support for or against selection of colleges according to career choice. If you are going to college, being involved is a perfect way to show that you are a well rounded person.

There are so many positives about being involved with extracurricular activities. The choice of activities is yours and most times a lot of fun. I still remember all of the good things that I learned from being a member of the cheerleading squad and the gymnastics team. Everyone knew me. I knew I had to keep my act together because I liked the idea of being in the spotlight. I felt a lot of school pride being on those teams. To have all eyes on me was great when I performed because the home scene was not exactly positive. I liked staying after school practicing and interacting with my friends on the different teams. My coaches encouraged me to concentrate in order to do my best and I did. Each time when I was injured, I wanted to quit, but my coach wouldn't let me. She always said, "Quitters never win and winners never quit. I can't let you quit. You must keep trying until you get it right"! I love her today for not allowing me to quit, because I have lived by that principle all of my college and adult life. That accolade made me a very determined person. So when there is something that I want, I stop at nothing within legal parameters to get it.

It felt so good to meet a challenge, to accomplish a goal, to be rewarded for doing some good for my school and to help a team become a winning team. There is great self-gratification and unity for participating in an extracurricular activity. By participating on a team, you learn how to be a team player and share ideas. If you shy away from joining a team, you lose out on a wonderful experience that helps you grow into a productive citizen.

I asked my students to share what they would do differently about participating in extracurricular activities if they could go back to high school. Some students admit that laziness prevented them from participating, and some admitted that over-involvement took control of them which caused them to fall short in academics. In other words, they did not balance their academics and extra-curricular activities.

The Lazzzy Disease

> "I participated in extracurricular activities in high school, but was lazy doing it. If I could go back to high school and prepare myself for college activities, I will first make sure I am dedicated to my choice of activities. Secondly, I would put more interest in doing them. Finally, I would make sure I stick with the activities to the end and make myself proud. If I could go back to high school, I would do a lot of preparing for possible scholarships. I found out that scholarships are not that hard to get."

Indecisive and Regretful

"I enjoyed my high school days back then. Those were times I will never forget, but there are some things that I wish I could change. I would change the amount of years that I played basketball because I could have been offered a scholarship from different colleges. Also, I wish that I had participated in more activities the school had instead of just going home each day and doing nothing. Reflecting back when I was in JROTC, I wished that I had spent more time playing ball instead, even if it was just for the two years that I had. Just thinking back to how much money I could have earned if I had stayed in JROTC and then gone to school and graduated. JROTC would have paid for my college education, and I would not have a loan to pay back like I am doing now."

Oh, my!!

When I was in high school, I should have participated in an extracurricular activity of some kind. College values extracurricular activities to help graduate productive students. I did not participate in any kind of extracurricular activity while in high school, so I have no competitive skills or desires now. I was just a deadbeat studious student. I think that if I knew extracurricular activities were popular in college, I would have participated in the Spanish club, school newspaper or something. Getting involved in the school community would have opened the avenue for me to better socialize while in college. All I do is go to class and do my homework. Boring!!!"

Distressed Overweight

"My eating habits in high school were terrible. I know now that what I was eating and not exercising was not at all good for me, but I did not know I was harming my future health. Yes, I heard it a million times. 'Watch what you eat and exercise.' Back then, it did not even occur to me that I was damaging my health and shortening my life. If I could go back, I would eat no more than 2000 calories a day and belong to some type of activity that allowed me active participation like: bat girl, tennis ball retriever, or discus thrower. If I could go back to high school days, I would exercise for at least 30 minutes every day with my friends. Now while in college, I stay in my room most days because I have no friends. Since I am 78 pounds overweight, I shy away from others. If only I knew back then what I know now, my life would be less complicated. Nevertheless, now that I know, I'm going to do everything I can to live a long, positively successful and healthy life."

Young Parent

"As far as extracurricular activities, I was on the volleyball team before I met Mr. Basketball Player. I put boys and supporting my male friend before my participating in volleyball. Mistake!! If nothing else, I could have done more community service projects in high school verses nothing. It not only would have made my college application look better, but it would have better prepared me for doing community service in college. In some college courses, I have to do community service to pass, and I'm just not used to that. I really don't have the time because I have a baby daughter to care for."

Hardheaded Athlete

"Other than school work, I wish I had listened better to my coaches while I was participating in sports. My football coach told me I had a lot of potential to play division 1 football because I had a lot of talent, but I was hardheaded and didn't listen. I thought they were just hyping me up, but now, I sit and think about what could have been. My academics slipped; therefore, I did not qualify for a scholarship. I did do okay in student government, winning Vice President of my class during my senior year. I also participated in the Future Farmers of America (FFA) and the Trojans Men's Club which is something like a big brother club, but I cannot participate in the one activity that I love the most, football."

Job-vs-Track Star

"Extracurricular activities are important in order to stay active and in shape. Whenever I was a little girl, my mom would keep me in some type of sport. I loved playing sports and being active. Once I became a junior in high school, I stopped everything completely. I thought I wanted a job more than anything in the world. My mom would say, 'Child, you have time for a job for the rest of your life.' I did not listen to her. I was making $10 an hour on my first job, and no one could tell me anything. If I could go back to high school, I would continue to run track like I truly wanted to and let my mom give me whatever little money she could."

Obedience Counts

"Extracurricular activities helped me groom myself into a well balanced individual; a talent I really needed to survive college life. However, my parents saw things differently and altogether failed to help me see the entire picture. I was forced to stop participating in all activities so that I could concentrate on my academic work. That was not a healthy decision, since with a lack of extra-curricular activities on my schedule, my body and brain became lazy. I should have stood up to my parents and assured them that I could do both, then maybe, I could have done satisfyingly better academically and succeed in sports. Instead, I was miserably bored and practically failed at both academics and football"

New Student

"I was not involved in any clubs while I was in high school, which I regret. I moved from a northern state to the south when I was in junior high school and if I was affiliated in more clubs and activities, I probably would have had an easier time adjusting to my new environment. I, also, wish I had joined more clubs because it would have helped to build my resume. It was hard for me to fit in, but if one is on a team of some kind and you have skills, you get respect and everyone gets to know you."

No Excuse

"I didn't make my time in high school really count and I'm really seeing the effects of that now. I think I would have stayed healthier participating in more extracurricular activities. I think it was my sophomore year in high school when I really stopped being involved in sports and being active in extracurricular activities. I regret it now because I am 30 lbs out of shape, and trying to get back in that state where I felt good about myself is going to take more work than I ever expected. If I had stayed active, I would be fine now and probably would be involved in some type of activity now in college. I have no excuse for why I stopped working out, but I must say, I regret it."

Oh Boy!!

"When I first got to high school, I was too much into the 'boys' thing. I should have been trying to join some type of sports team around school. During my sophomore year in high school, I was a cheerleader, but I did not like the varsity coach, so I did not try out the next year. I should have not let that get in the way of me joining a team. During my junior and senior year, I played volleyball.

I should of started playing volleyball in the ninth grade; then maybe, I would have been playing on a full scholarship in college. If I could rewind time, there are more things I would change before coming to college."

Popularity Counts

"During high school, I was very athletic and very involved in a lot of activities and clubs around school. I was very well-known as being loud, crazy, and outspoken during school, and everyone knew me. My extra activities were soccer, basketball, track and tennis. I focused more on sports than my books. I was the type of person who would give up anything just so I could play ball or run at the meets. My coaches made us get focused more on our work, because if we did not meet the grade point average, we could not play. Most people, including myself, were to stay on top of our game during the sport season. Then, we had a reason to stay focused on our work because if not, everyone knew the consequence would be no playing time or we would get put off the team."

Extracurricular Tips for High School Students from College Students

- Whichever activity or sport you decide to participate in, give it your all, but do not neglect your academic work. Keep in mind that you are a student first, then an athlete.

- Strive to become a leader at whatever you do. You are a student leader because your peers look up to you. At all times, show your best manners.

- If you wish to get an athletic scholarship, keep in mind that your athletic abilities will get you in college, but your academic achievement will keep you there.

- Get involved in as many extracurricular activities as you can handle without neglecting your academic work. Be determined to let your talents shine.

- Engaging in a variety of extracurricular activities will help you to narrow the field of prospective careers. You may be unsure of what to do for the rest of your life, but you will surely know what you <u>do not</u> want to do.

- The activities in which you participate in high school could be the beginning of a career or could lead to something you could get more involved in when you get to college and have something to add to your resume.

- Some activities offer opportunities for you to travel and meet people in other school environments and communities. On these occasions, you should positively represent your school. Be seen and not heard.

- Practice applies to sports and academics. There are times when the team practice strategies and the teacher gives homework to practice basic skills. Find time to practice on your own so that you may become exceptional.

- Stay focused on your goals. Do not let "you" stand in your way of fulfilling a passion for the activity you love. If you work hard at it, it will pay off for you.

- Depending on the choice of extracurricular activity, it could possibly lead to a part-time job tutoring a child who has the same interest as you.

CHAPTER 5

KNOW WHERE YOU ARE IN THE RELATIONSHIP

Relationships are the true togetherness of persons who have bonded over a period of time. Relationships have an impact on our lives, and we have an impact on relationships. We call those persons we relate to well, "friends." Friends share the same thoughts and inclinations about an idea or issue. Friends wish each other happiness and prosperity. Friends are happy for your achievements. There is some sort of interdependence on each other. Friends put you ahead of themselves, within reason, and friends trust and believe in you. A true friend can make you believe in yourself if needed.

Developing relationships with people we meet and those we know is imperative. Choosing the people we want to have as close friends and associates is an extremely important decision. While in high school, consider finding friends who are much like you, who motivate you and who inspire you to be successful. That is, choose persons who have some of the same beliefs as you and view the world as a stepping stone to achieving success and not just a place to exist.

I have always heard that in order to have a friend, you must know how to be a friend. This is kind of a catch 22. Well, do we just automatically know how to be a friend if you have never had a friend. I found meaning through the words of scripture, "do unto to others as you would have them do unto you" and "love thy neighbors as thyself." Believe me, there are a lot of sayings out there that could help add meaning to being a friend. How about "never kick a man when he is down" or "if you can't say anything good about a person, don't say anything" or "friends don't let friends drive drunk." I am sure that even as young as you are, you have heard your parents or grandparents use some cliché that could stir you in the right direction with the people that you meet and want to hang out with.

On the other hand, "take heed to warning." If you are warned about a so called friend, step back and take a good look at the relationship and whether or not the person adds meaning to your life. Sometimes you might be too close to the mirror to see what others can see about your friend. So step back and take another look; weigh the pros and the cons. I guarantee you that the signs are right there before you. You should not try to become friends with a person who exhibits any of the following: domineering nature, a negative outlook on life, disrespect towards others, and disregard for your thoughts, feelings and ideas. Just try to be acquaintances or associates or nothing at all. You do not have to be friends, associates or even acquaintances with everyone who calls you homey, homeboy or my man. Do not try to treat those persons like close friends or confidants. It won't work and somebody is always left holding the "bag" (in trouble). Guess who? You! When the going gets tough, the tough get going, and you won't have a clue as to what hit you. If you hang with someone who will do the kinds of things to get in trouble, wrong one. If you hang with someone who is dishonest about their participation in the activity, wrong one.

My nephew gave an associate a ride one night to a nearby sports grill where college students congregated. They were around college age and wanted to attract some girls. Upon their arrival, they went their separate ways. The guy who rode with my nephew decided to rob some females on the sidewalk, but the guys had been seen coming and leaving together, so they were all thrown in jail. Furthermore, my nephew served a one-year jail sentence, because he didn't know the hitchhiker's real name. When asked by the police for the name of the guys he came and went with, he only knew the nickname, Rob. There is nothing more ridiculous than getting in trouble with someone whom you don't even know.

A friend of the family's son went out with some so-called friends that he had not seen in years. He came home from college for the summer and wanted to hang out with the same old friend that he had not seen since high school graduation. He had a job at one of the local convenient stores by day and hung out with friends some nights. Upon the direction of one of the so called friends, he was dared to rob other students who attended the local university. He did not have a weapon, but the guy with him had a BB gun. Well, he was identified, and faces charges of 20 years in prison for his participation. The hand of one is the hand of all.

Be very selective of the friends you keep to run with and the ones you throw away. You are sometimes known by association, "birds of a feather hang together." Look at it this way: pigeons fly with pigeons, geese fly with geese and crows fly with crows. You will not see them flying with each other. That's why you are known by the acts of the people you select to befriend. Now, that may not necessarily hold true for fraternities and sororities unless that Greek organization has a reputation for selecting candidates who are willing to act as the rest of them. Why would anyone deliberately select an organization for membership whose members are known to be notorious or "bad asses." In my opinion, that is a jail sentence waiting to happen. For instance: gangs in some communities have recruited or some persons voluntarily joined, because they were singled out. If you learn how to select the right kind of people to keep in your company, then it will be easier to find law abiding friends and activities that attract good law-abiding citizens as organizational members as you go through high school and enter college. You learn how not to put yourself at risk of becoming a victim of circumstance.

Relationships where two people have been intimate are sometimes the hardest to break away from, especially if this is the first person you were intimate with or there is now a baby involved. Listen to your parents and elders as they have been through some situations that they wish to protect you from experiencing. Abstinence is the best way to survive a relationship in high school and college. Get to know a person. Go with your gut feelings. If your gut feelings tell you that this is not the right person for you, then move on. If the other person tells you that you are not the person for him or her, take it at face value and move on. Stalking and falling victim is not the way to show someone that you care about them and allowing someone to victimize you does not mean you love them or they love you. It's a crime in the making.

My students shared with me some things they would change about relationships if they could go back to high school.

Teacher-student relationship

"Though I had great relationships with my peers, I didn't have strong relations with the teachers who taught me. Now that I am thinking back, I should have formed close relationships in high school like I have in college. These teachers could have been networks that could have gotten me more places than I've gotten myself. The relationship that I had with friends, I would never alter. I hung out with a group of people whose academic goals were similar to mine. Everybody I knew wanted to do better than the people we lived around, while setting examples for people we knew could do better but never had the encouragement."

Popular and Popular

"I wish I had focused more of my attention on those who may not have had as much in common with me as I thought, but who may have been a good person. Even though I was fairly popular and never had a grudge with anyone, I should have expanded my horizons more with other groups. Not just the people who were within my comfort level. This is also true with my relationships with the opposite sex. Most of the time, I decided to date someone who was as popular as me: cheerleader, "A" student, with the in-crowd and who others thought I should date. Instead of breaking away from what others thought, I allowed myself to be pigeonholed into dating guys who were popular athletes and well-known. I regret not getting to know other guys who showed genuine interest in me and not just for show and what was expected."

Please Help!!

"I had a problem with asking for help. Sometimes when I needed help, I would be too ashamed to ask for it, so I let my grades drop continuously. After school was out I would go hang out with friends before and after practice. Now I see that I could have spent this time getting help and getting my work done. There were after school programs that offered to help with school work, but I chose not to do anything that would benefit me. I can also say that I enjoyed high school years with my friends. We were all dummies together. I would not say that I did completely bad, but playing sports was my main priority in high school. I was still able to attend college and play football. My college life is much different than high school because while playing football, I still get my work done and I ask for help."

Growing Pains

"I should have been more open to meeting new people and not just staying around the friends that I already know and have, because it helps a lot to meet new people in college not only socially but for school too. As far as relationships with a girlfriend, I really don't think I would have done anything differently because you learn more things and run into different problems as you grow. I should have learned to gain a relationship with my teachers because it is very helpful if you have a good relationship with your teachers in college."

College Prep, Teachers

"My relationship with my teachers was fair. In high school, we all had our best teachers. I never had a teacher that just gave me a grade. Realizing that I had to do my work helped prepare me for college. If I needed a better understanding about a particular lesson, all of my teachers had time to help me. All I had to do was ask. One of my teachers told me to try college first when I told him that my focus was the military. I had bad relationships with a few teachers, but most saw the potential in me. Basically, my relationship with my teachers prepared me for college."

"Cool" Kids

"Most of my friends in high school were athletes, you know, cool people like me. I just wished I was surrounded by the right people and smarter people who could motivate me to do the right thing. I made some bad mistakes hanging around the "cool" kids. I participated in recreational and leisure activities that school offered. Those activities really helped me socially in life. I just wish I knew in high school what I know now in college about relationships."

Friends and Boyfriends/Girlfriends

"I see now that people change over the years, and the ones who were my friends in high school don't talk to me now. I feel like I every day in life is a lesson way but then again, I feel like every day in life is a lesson learned whether we know it or not. I thank the fake people for showing me their true colors. I have moved on from that even though it hurt. On top of that, the four year relationship with this guy taught me that there are more fish in the sea. I wouldn't say that the time was wasted because it wasn't all bad. I learned a great lesson from this person. Even though I wish I could change a lot of things, I am moving on through my journey of life."

Networking Wish

"I was satisfied with the personal decision to not be in an intimate relationship. However, I should have done more networking which I had learned to do once I got to college. This would have been good to help me start college knowing how to handle myself with persons of any stature. Each area needed to be polished and would have better prepared me for college."

Need More!

"The thing I would change most with relationships would be to have more relationships. I consider myself a social misfit. I did not have many relationships in high school, and I still don't have many in college. I stayed in the house most of the time. If I was a social person, I would know how to choose what kind of persons I want to be with and what type of people I want to be around."

Relationship Tips for High School Students from College Students

- Dump all excess relationship baggage before coming to college.

- Listen to responsible friends who tell you about what they see in the person you call a friend.

- Learn good verbal and written communication skills. Say what you mean and mean what you say.

- Be willing to compromise so you do not always get the short end of the stick. Know when to be humble. Be willing to admit when you are wrong and speak up for something you strongly believe in.

- Do not get mixed up with lust and love. Take the time to get to know someone before getting intimate.

- To gain trust from friends, be honest and truthful at all times.

- Be yourself. Do not try to be someone you are not.

- Once you detect a "fair weather" friend, move on.

- Develop a relationship with your teachers and college professors so they will understand what you are about, and you will get an understanding of what is expected of you in class.

CHAPTER 6

BEING BULLIED-VS-
BEING PICKED ON

The Magnitude of Being Picked-on

Everyone has been picked-on by loved ones and seemingly, the older you are and the longer you've known someone, the longer the teasing can go on. Friends usually know how far to take the teasing to push a button or to make you lift an eyebrow. Wikipedia has described teasing as having many meanings. "Teasing comes in two major forms, playful and hurtful. When teasing is playful and friendly, and especially when it is reciprocal, teasing can be regarded as flirting" (Wikipedia, 2012). People get teased about many things: appearance, clothes and shoes, eye glasses, body size and/or shape, attitude, being smart or not so smart, inability to play sports, reading aloud, special friend's features, and the list could go on forever.

Most times, teasing tends to be innocent, and the person doing the teasing doesn't have to think about the attitude or the mental state of the person he/she is teasing. It is playful, fun, acceptable teasing. A lot of times, teasing is a conversation piece. Someone may be attracted to another person and use teasing as a way to get noticed or use teasing as a way to brighten a moment if the feelings are mutual. On the other hand, the teaser could be someone who is totally disliked by the person being teased, and it could be an avenue for trouble which leads to an argument or some violent act. Teasers usually make their intention known by how they say what is said. Everyone can distinguish between the sound of a friendly voice and make the difference in the tone of a voice that is trying to embarrass one's spirit.

For the person receiving the tease, it could be hurtful. Sometimes we do not know how a person feels about the issue they are being teased about. The response from the victim will give some indication of how the tease is accepted. A lot of nicknames come about through teasing. Once my friends tried to call me "pug" because my nose was shaped real funny, but when I ignored them, it went away like nothing ever started. When I put up a big fuss about being called "Mabel," that stuck like glue on a stamp. I had to keep telling myself that I tease others and others are going to tease me. I learned that on my bad days, I did not play teasing very well and I teased others back very critically. On my good days, I viewed teasing as acceptable and the teaser was a person with a sense of humor and I participated.

People tease for many reasons and about many things, but the person being teased has a choice to make: either to laugh it off or get upset. Ignoring the teaser may convince that person to stop. You can simply say "and" or "so" each time the teasing starts. Keep in mind that the teaser may just be trying to get you to take notice because of an attraction. Sometimes people do not know any other way to show feelings towards another person or may not like the fact that they are attracted to a person who is not interested in him or her. Hara Marano indicated in her article, How to Poke Fun, that there was a fine line between aggression and play. "Teasing teaches us the elements of communication. It is fundamentally ambiguous, so it forces us to pay attention to all aspects of an interaction in order to decipher its meaning" (Marano, 2008). Always remember that teasing is associated with bullying, and your response will cause the teasing to stop or to continue, so keep cool when you are teased. Try not to be offended or embarrassed by what the teaser says.

I grew up in the 60's and 70's when everyone was teased playing the "dirty dozen" which was and still is the "your mama" teaser of a life time. In playing the dozens, people drew attention to things people said or thought about your mom and a lot of emotional fires were lit. For example: "Yo mama is so big, she has to go outside to turn around in the house." "Yo mama is so short, she has to duck to play bridge." "Yo mama is so ugly, I thought she belong to the Baboon family." But here is one that would start a fight. Let's say the dad deserted the home and after a year or so, he came back. If someone playing the dozens, told a male child from that family "Yo mama is so dumb, that's why she let yo daddy come back to beat yo ass," that would surely start a fight. The teaser would know that some of what he said was factual and was intended to hurt the feelings of the person spoken to; especially, if the person who is being teased did not have any hurtful facts to throw back.

The Magnitude of Being Bullied

Childhood and adolescent bullying has now become a major health problem in the Western world and is closely associated with suicide, the third leading cause of mortality in the United States for adolescents. Bullying has been defined as "an aggressive behavior in which individuals in a dominant position intend to cause mental and/or physical suffering to others" (Olweus, 1994). Bullying is a learned behavior that could manifest in any one person, depending on the situation. Moreover, insecurity and low self-esteem are usually what triggers a bully's behavior. Researchers and students tend to include physical and emotional abuse in a true definition of bullying. According to Brent Harger, assistant professor at Albright College, "many students view bullying as a false dichotomy in which others are either 'bullies' or 'non-bullies,' but they must fit that label all of the time" (Science Daily, 2009).

All students have been "picked on" by family and friends, but the experiences of children that identify with bullying behaviors include: verbal bullying (insulting, name calling, telling lies, threatening, etc,), physical bullying (pushing, grabbing, hitting, punching, biting, slapping, etc.), and exclusion (being rejected, being ignored, being talked over, etc.). As a result, researchers might label a student's action as bullying, but students might see that same behavior as non-bullying because a lot of other factors need to be considered about the person considered as the bully.

The literature is clear that victims may experience many health related consequences as a result of being bullied. "Victimized children are reported to have clinical problems, including bed—wetting, sleep difficulties, anxiety, depression, school phobia, feelings of insecurity, and unhappiness at school" (Olweus, 1994). The consequences can be short-term or long-term depending on the mental stability and the health condition of the victim. Consequences from being bullied also include: poor school attendance, lower grades, increased stress/worrying, fewer friends, violent behavior towards self, others or the school, and increased thoughts of suicide.

Cyber Bullying

With the improvement of technology, more and more children are becoming intelligent technologists and at an earlier age. Searching the internet and visiting site after site and participating in World Wide Web activities, has led to children losing contact with reality. With the introduction of Facebook, Twitter, text messaging, and even e-mail, children learned how to send instant messages to friends. Cyber bullying is sending messages to those persons who are not very well-liked by the person sending the message. It is an act of retaliation about something.

Cyber bullying has become an increasing public concern in view of the reported cases of youth suicides that have been reported. A recent cross-sectional study indicated that "experience with cyber victimization is associated with an increase in depression, suicidal ideation, and suicide attempts" (Brunstein, et. al., 2007). Both girls and boys who were bullied through email or internet were reported as associated with depression and suicidal ideation.

Avoid cyber bullying by doing a few things: 1) Change your email address, and do not give it to strangers. 2) Do not open email from persons you do not know. 3) Report strange behavior to the carrier of the person sending irresponsible email messages. 4) Report the person to your parents and the local authorities. 5) Refrain from participating in activities that might haunt you later in life like: posting nude or half nude pictures, making ugly responses on

Twitter and Facebook, or drawing attention to yourself by sharing what you will do or have done.

Always keep the golden rule in mind: "Do unto others as you would have them do unto you." Try very hard not to write ugly words about someone and try not to give anyone a reason to write anything about you. Mind your own business unless you are writing something to save a person's life. Remember, cyber bullying is a retaliation of something done prior to the bullying message being sent; for sure, victims are clothes-lined or hit on the blindside, but what hurts so much is the messages are mass communicated.

Bullying and the Law

The punishment must fit the crime. Is it against the law to bully another person? Several questions need to be answered about bullying and suicide when it comes to the punishment for the person who is responsible for the death of another person. Should the person who pushes another to the edge that ends life be punished? What should the punishment be for someone who pulls a prank on a friend or a roommate or a targeted person of questionable sexual orientation? Should anyone be held responsible for offensive messages distributed through cyberspace or circulated through text messages, Twitter and Facebook? Does someone have the right to publish derogatory stories about another person without consequences?

Authors agree that "public humiliation and sexual orientation can be an especially deadly blend" (Schwartz, 2010). With the increase in multi-media, so is the increase in cyber bullying over sexual orientation even in children as young as 13 years old. The ultimate question in all of this is should the fact that a victim committed suicide as a direct result from being bullied end with the bully being held responsible for the way the victim responded. Prosecutors are throwing the book at face-to-face bullies and cyber bullies as well. Prosecutors are investigating each case and treating bullying as a bias crime with a possible punishment of up to 10 years in prison.

Detection and Protection

If you find yourself confronted by a bully, ask yourself what you did to be attractive to the bully. Sometimes, you don't have to do anything for a bully to single you out. You could be victimized because you are someone who takes care of their own business or in the wrong place at the wrong time. Maybe, you have seen too much or know something that could get the bully in trouble. If at any time you are confronted by a bully for whatever the reason, inform the people with whom you have established a relationship and trust someone to be there for you: parents, teachers, and school administrators. Next, file a report with the local authorities: school security, campus police, or city/county police. Do not wait to see if there will be a second incident because there will be a second incident. It is just a matter of time and convenience before the second run-in. Seek immediate help after the first incident. Bullies will dare you not to tell, but for your safety, let adults know who has approached you in an unacceptable manner. For your protection, give all of the person's identifying information to the adults who know and will protect you.

CHAPTER 7

WHAT OR WHO MOTIVATES YOU?

In case you do not know what I mean by motivation, let me share a definition that may be easy to keep in mind as you read this chapter. Motivation is a force, a stimulus or an influence of some kind that drives you to do the things that you decide to do. The force, stimulus or influence can be negative or positive and can come from within you or from someone/something around you. At this point in life, you may not know what motivates you to do the things you do. Respectfully, I hope your parents are on the scene and helping you to become the intrinsically motivated person that you will need to become by the time you reach college. Parents cannot go to college with you. Parents can advise, feud, fuss, discuss, tell, threaten, or even cuss you out, but they cannot make you do anything. You will make most of the decisions on your own once you get to college. So get ready. Practice now analyzing the pros and cons of your decisions.

A child is not born intrinsically motivated. Intrinsic motivation comes out of need or some value system that has been taught. A child who has been sheltered, cradled or taught to rely on parents for every waking breath is not likely to become intrinsically motivated or to be an assertive person who strives for excellence. That person will be slightly lethargic in acting and thinking, unlike that person who learned to make life and death decisions early in life. Children who are left to fend for themselves early in life, along with guidance at school from teachers and counselors, become intrinsically motivated to succeed in life. These children want what they could not have at home. They have a point to prove to the world. They want everyone to know that they are worthy of belonging to a group of high rollers.

As a child, I was intrinsically motivated. I wanted to be the best at everything I did and still do. My teachers encouraged me. Since I modeled myself after the formally recognized gifted and talented children at my school, I came out okay. I am driven by achievement. I feel successful when I help others to become successful. During my grade school years, I was battered and made to believe that I would not amount to much, but I never believed that. Even as a child, I knew that I was the type of person who could say or who could determine the outcome of my life. I had great teachers, and I listened to what they told the gifted students. I had two teachers who actually told me and made me believe that one day I would be okay in the adult arena if I kept my head on straight. I grew up trying to prove to everyone who thought that I would not amount to anything that I was going to be about something.

I was the "black sheep" (one least liked or expected to succeed) in my family. At the age of fourteen, I had a disagreement with my dad that led to him telling me that he would not give me anything else as long as I lived. Well, he lived up to his words. At the time, I did not care. I just wanted the battering to stop. By accepting the fact that he would not help me, he began to brain-wash me about not being wealthy, healthy, or a clean independent citizen. I was supposed to be a high school dropout who lived on government assistance with a lot of children living in a dump. But to his dismay, my dad's words motivated me to do just the opposite of what he proposed for me.

In the '60's, children did not have a social security number (SS#) until the age of 18 or if they got a job at the age of 16 or 17. I got my SS# at the age of 14 when I started working in what was known as the 5 and 10 cent store (comparable to dollar general store) in the shoe repair department. I hated that job with a passion, but I loved having a job to help me pay for my school lunch, school supplies and a few pieces of clothes. I hated picking up and giving back people's dirty, stinky shoes to be repaired, but I kept that after school job for nearly two years, then I got into sports. The job paid 90 cents an hour, and I usually worked 25-30 hours a week. I was hired as the cashier to help Mr. Bing, the shoe repairman who weighed nearly 400 pounds and had problems with mobility. To accommodate his disability, the store hired a cashier/helper to give people their shoes and to get shoes while customers waited to have their shoes repaired.

When business was slow, Mr. Bing would pay me to go to his house to help his wife clean their apartment. The wife was in perfect health, but here was an opportunity to have a "Black" housekeeper at the company's expense. So he gave me round trip bus fare to his house and gave me ten extra hours per week for helping his wife clean up their two bedroom 800 square foot apartment. I don't know which I despised more, going to Mr. Bing's house or touching those stinky shoes.

The next year, the new physical education teacher started a gymnastics team, and I found peace and joy in being a member of that team and the track team. She was Caucasian and came to our school at the time when the South was desegregating schools. She was young and so compassionate, always encouraging us to keep at it until we succeeded. Well, I applied all of her coaxing and persistence to my life journey. I couldn't work after school and practice with the team so I was broke for a while even though I did work some weekends. I had friends who shared with me if they had money and sometimes just took lunch money from my dad's change jar that he kept in his bedroom closet. Whenever I asked him for money, I never got it, and my mom acted as if she was afraid to cross him by letting him know that she gave me money.

My next job was working at my dad's community grocery store for the summer for $15.00 a week. When it was time to be paid, he told me that I needed to pay for room and board, so he kept my pay. When school started, he gave me some of it to pay for my school clothes and a pair of shoes. Well, needless to say that really taught me how to save and pay cash for my needs. Work, put up the pay check and spend the money later when you need it. I still practice that principle today.

I had several jobs after that. After graduation, I went to New York to work for the summer. I found work in a notebook factory where I worked for several weeks until the manager got fresh and I quit. I next worked in a McCrory's 5 and 10 cent store for the rest of the summer. I saved up enough money to pay for my tuition at college and buy a few new pieces of clothes. My next summer job was at a doll factory back home, then a rug fiber company and lots of baby-sitting during my free time. All of these hourly waged jobs motivated me to stay in school, get a degree and find a professional job making some real money. I followed the plan and reached my goal. I would often feel a little rush to show everyone who knew me and my story that I was going to be successful and not that person that my dad and teachers predicted I would become.

I knew when I was in the 7th grade that I was going to be a teacher. When I met my homeroom/English teacher, Mrs. Susan B. Freeman, I wanted to be just like her. She was considerate, compassionate, honest, fair and like no other teacher I ever had at the time. I loved what she stood for. She would even come through my neighborhood to see if I needed a ride to school on very cold and wet days. She had the loveliest spirit in a teacher that I ever experienced. So I wanted to be an English teacher, and I made "A's" in English. Then there was Mr. Colie Rayford, my physical education teacher who taught me how to move and control my body in the many sport skills that he taught. I loved physical education (PE), and when I started taking his classes, I thought I had died and gone to heaven. You see, I did not have PE until the seventh grade. I always had my uniform clean and ready for class. Mr. Rayford was a strong disciplinarian, and he was so organized. I often wondered how he kept boys and girls straight when he could not go in the girls locker room, but he managed well for over 40 years. He also introduced his classes to dance and how to prepare for sporting events.

I was torn between being an English teacher or a physical education teacher. In high school, you might know that the English teachers who taught me did not inspire me, but my physical education teacher, Mrs. Francis Ferrene was the bomb. Mrs. Ferrene made me a champion gymnast in two years. I competed and placed 2nd overall in the regional Olympic tryouts in the summer of 1970. Thus, I knew that I wanted to be a physical education teacher, but my favorite disciplinarian was my French teacher, Mrs. Urusha Spigner. She kept everybody straight, even the principal.

I said all of that to say that you should not let anyone define you. You will meet people on your way to adulthood who will motivate, inspire and influence you and the decisions you make. It is your decision to determine what you want to do for the rest of your life and in your career. Make wise decisions now! If you decide to work for the city collecting trash, just be good at it. Learn the trade and what you need to do in order to gain recognition with honors, because you did a job like no one else could. If you want to become a doctor, pilot, architect or scientist, explore the internet to learn fundamental background knowledge before you start high school. If you are already in high school, start as soon as possible gaining the basic skills for your choice of a career. Visit the website of your college choice to see if your preferred major is offered. If not, find another college. You do not want to attend a school just because of the town or your family has adopted the school due to the football or the basketball team. Get focused and stay focused until you reach your goal. You will go far in life if you are intrinsically motivated and aspire to become all that you can be, instead of limiting yourself to what someone else wants you to become.

Find someone in your field of interest, and ask that person to mentor you or to have you as an intern. This will give you insight as to what it takes to get the job done. For instance, babysitting gave me insight so that I could determine whether I wanted to undertake teaching as a career. There are many college students who have no idea as to what they want to choose as a major, so they are not prepared mentally or academically. They fail in school, because they have not settled on a career and are not working diligently in that career area. By their junior year in college, students start changing majors. Finally, they either decide what they most want a degree in, or their grade point average dictates what degree they can actually graduate with.

CHAPTER 8

HELP IS AT YOUR FINGERTIPS

Just like in the **Wizard of Oz**, Dorothy always had the power to go home. All she had to do was click her heels together and focus her dream on going home. You have the power to succeed by seeking help when needed. You cannot go through life alone. Surviving is so much easier when you go through a storm with someone else. Luther Van Dross wrote in his song, "I would rather be with you in a storm than safe at home alone." You are an amazing machine with the power to do anything you please within the realm of the law. All of us are put together to depend on one another. The ultimate plan is to seek each other for help. Ask your parents, grandparents, siblings, peers, teachers, associates, friends, counselors, administrators or neighbors for assistance if you need help.

Some of my students wrote that they refused to ask for help while in high school, and this is one of the reasons why they are having problems in college. Once you get used to asking for help, you will continue to seek help. On the other hand, if you try to make it through life and never ask for help, you will continue the same pattern of not asking for help even when you need help the most in life. Instead of viewing asking for help as a sign of weakness, look at it as a way of making you stronger.

Those people with the ultimate masculine pride or the diva ego will think they have all the answers. It is difficult to get through to them no matter what the evidence. There was a time when I was in college that I never wanted to go to my professors to ask for help, especially when I attended the University of South Carolina, then a predominately white school with very few African-American students. As a matter of fact, I was the only African-American female in my graduate school classes in the mid 1980s. I did not want my professors to know what I did not know. In my heart, I thought they would grade me based on what they believed I did not know. So, I took chances and studied with other students.

I have actually talked with students who thought they were too high-class to go to tutoring sessions. I have held tutoring sessions for my classes for students who were not doing so well and even on the verge of failing, and some of those students did not show up for help. Whom do you look to for help academically or with relationships? There were times when I needed help with a relationship more than help academically and felt a real need to talk with someone who understood what I was going through. When other people think negatively of you or reject you, it can be devastating to the point where you hear absolutely nothing while sitting in class.

Sometimes we cannot see that we need to put ourselves first. Regardless of what you might think, you have to think more of yourself than others think of you. People do things to rattle your thinking. Remember this: if you think you have an emotional problem, then you can talk yourself into showing emotional symptoms. If you have an emotional problem, you can think yourself into acting as normal as anyone else. I have seen it. There was a student in my class who was registered with the University as "special needs"; actually, he was listed as having a learning disability. He could out-think any of our so-called "normal students" and was more organized than I am. Thus, the power of the mind over body assists you in taking the straight and narrow road. Somewhere I remember hearing my teachers say, "If you think you can, you can. If you think you can't, you can't."

Let me say, you have your parents to help you whenever you fall short of solutions and ideas. I may have had some troubles at home, but home taught me to take care of myself, because you never know when someone might decide to stop caring about you. The average parent will love you unconditionally. You can ask your parents or guardian for help with anything you need. Parents may not know exactly all of the pros and cons of your situation, but they will interpret the situation and get you whatever you need to be successful. I am a parent. I would do almost anything to help my child be successful at almost anything he decides would suit him. Stop right now, and go test your parent. Ask for an opinion about a career you are interested in pursuing, and look for the smile that says "thank you for involving me." Parents want to help. If your parents have not said what they want you to be when you grow up, it's because they want you to tell them. Do not be afraid to share that early in life, even though it might change several times before you make a final decision. Just keep in mind that you have the right to decide. You know your parents, and your parents know you. True story: seemingly, everyday my parents said, "Y'all going to college. All my children are going to college." All six of us did go to the college of our financial choice. My siblings and I knew that our parents had expectations for us, so we developed expectations for ourselves. Parents will always be there to advise you. You just have to know how to accept and use that advice.

Do you have grandparents? Your grandparents may very well be bigger advocates for you than your parents. As a grandparent, all I have to do is know that my grandbaby is in need of something, and I am off to pick it up. Your grandparents are probably the same. Grandparents realize how much it took for them to get to where they considered themselves as being comfortable: financially, socially and religiously. A rigid grandparent, from the school of hard knocks, will have you do it yourself to appreciate what you accomplish, perhaps even more than your parents would. A trusting, "believe in you" grandparent will be there every inch of the way until you achieve success, without a shadow of a doubt that you will fulfill your dreams. Don't believe me? Then take the grandparent test. Stop reading, and call your grandparent this minute. Tell your grandparents what you want to be when you grow up, and listen to all of the good free advice you get. Weigh it carefully, and thank them when you're done. Keep in mind that your grandparents may be willing to help you financially, even if in no other way. Be nice, because while the advice might seem ancient, you have to respect the fact that your grandparents are from a totally different generation than you and your siblings. But grandparents mean well and are great listeners.

A loving neighbor or church member would be so happy to have you ask for help about anything. In my neighborhood, when I grew up, my neighbors and church members were part of the extended family. They reported to my parents and grandparents anything they thought was suspicious. My parents knew where I was and what I was doing before I got home. Neighbors and some church members today don't do the extended family thing. If you are an outgoing person and you know your neighbors or your friends' parents, then you know which ones you can trust to help you when you share your heartfelt thoughts. Neighbors today do not know each other and children do not try to get to know who lives next door. Get to know your neighbors and church members. Invite them to your school or a community function. They, too, need to know who lives next door. If you need a character letter to get in college, your neighbor would be a great person to ask.

Having a friend or a really close associate while in high school is the greatest thing ever. All students need someone they can at least share some good and bad times with. All students need someone to study with or talk to for some calming words when anger sets in. Sometime we do not realize how close we are to someone until that person is no longer in our lives. Nurture your friendships. Make your own decisions, but know that it helps to release stress when you have someone close to you to share your inner thoughts, ideas and beliefs. A really good friend who believes in you will tell you the truth, even if the truth is not what you really want to hear. A really good friend will not let you do something that is totally out of character for you. That friend is someone you should be willing to listen to, because you know he or she won't just tell you what you want to hear. If you don't have a really good friend, start finding a friend by being a friend.

At school, you have teachers, coaches or counselors who will welcome you into their office and listen to you disclose any conflict you have, whether it is a conflict with yourself or with another person. I share with my students to be careful how they treat others, because you never know when or where they may break down from the pressures of school work, home relations and/or team associations. Try not to be so distant that you cannot share your feelings with others. Students who rise to the point of being held in high esteem by others and those who go unnoticed at school are at high risk of snapping when things go wrong or when feeling pressured. Have you thought of befriending a person in your class or at your school whom you know is introverted, quiet and always alone? Teachers, coaches and counselors expect a lot from and respect their students. Develop a relationship with an adult at school whom you can talk to when the going gets tough.

Many students get a part-time job when in high school. So did my son, but he soon found out that taking AP classes and working a part-time job was not a good formula for passing high school and playing sports. He was on the band, playing baseball, taking advanced college level classes, working at Bi-Lo and handling a full load of other classes. When his grade point average dropped, he decided he needed to concentrate on just school and band. Part-time jobs can really take away quality time from a student and the family. There are no guarantees that you will have people to confide in at the part-time job. Forget that job unless it is absolutely necessary. If they are willing, allow your parents to take care of you by providing the things you need. Most students who want a job have parents who are strict about frivolous spending. So the teenager goes out to find a job. Some need a job because their parents cannot afford all of the high school expenses. Whatever the reason, be aware of the fact that a part-time job takes away time from your academics and relationships. In my opinion, it is never a good idea to take your problems on the job. You won't do a good job on the job if you have baggage.

Trouble seems to follow some youth. So if you know a special police officer or parole officer whom you can spend time with and share some of your life adventures, then do so. Officers have great conversation about how to stay out of trouble with the law and how to get along with others. They can tell you where to go when the going gets tough. Officers have a lot of experience working with the public and can give you a good calculated guess as to what will happen when you pick the wrong people to befriend. They can tell you what will possibly happen when you let others think for you. Officers will be the first to tell you that trouble is so easy to get into, but so hard to get out of. So stay on the straight and narrow road. Always do the right thing, because that's the right thing to do.

Are you a member of a special youth organization? There are the scouts, recreational teams, youth clubs, church ministries, youth political groups or other after school programs. All of these organizations have leaders who are more than willing to serve teens. They are usually volunteers and are there because they choose to be there. Most leaders of the organizations are somebody's parent and want the best for young people. Many of the organizations were started to get and keep kids off the street or from being home alone. Leaders of youth organizations can serve as a mentor or role model to help you beat the odds or get ahead. So instead of a part-time job, think about a youth organization that will train you to pass it forward.

Now, I saved the best for last. If you have a special friend and feel love sparks between the two of you, so that you cannot resist texting or calling or wanting to see each other every minute of the day, then you may have someone who will listen to all of your good news and bad news. Most young people tend to see someone close to them as a person they will keep in their lives forever. That may or may not happen. The expectations of a relationship can take a toll on the couple involved. Take the time to get to know the person you like and with much communication, you two may fall in love or become a habit to each other. Keep the windows of your mind open for the unexpected, and always remember that everyone is entitled to his or her own opinion.

On a strictly personal note, you are responsible for your own happiness and solving your own problems, or you can sit back and let them eat at you until your problems tear down your self-esteem. When issues arise, keep in mind that you must remain calm in order to think of possible solutions. It is good to have someone you can rely on to be there for you to talk things over. Set high expectations for yourself, and believe that you are number one in your life. Have respect for *yourself*, and others will respect you. Others are going to talk about you, so give them something good and exciting to talk about.

CHAPTER 9

DISCIPLINE YOURSELF

The word "discipline" is one of the strongest words in the English language. It has several connotations that overlap and are confusing at times. Discipline could stand out as meaning "being punished or penalized for actions" or "showing self-control" or "choosing an area of study." No matter which way you look at discipline, discipline is in your hands. The choice belongs to you.

In preparation for college, make sure you keep your school disciplinary record clean. Once at college, you are on your honor to do the right thing because that is the right thing to do. No person will be there looking over your shoulder 24-7 to make sure you are doing your work, minding your own business and leaving other people's things alone. You take with you the moral teachings of your parents and grandparents. You are expected to take that code of honor with you everywhere you go. Hopefully, your parents will have instilled in you all of the right things to do, as they expect you to do the right thing while away from home. As you matriculate through high school, will you be able to get through high school without a discipline record, or will you have some crazy-acting stuff on your record? As I mentioned earlier, no one can make you do anything; the choice is yours. Discipline records indicate whether you have self-control and are able to make good decisions. Records tell what decisions you made that you cannot take back. The discipline record tells how many times you made the same wrong decision and how often. Your record speaks loudly about your character. It tells what kinds of things you are willing to get in trouble about. It tells if you get in trouble alone or with others. It tells if you are a victim or a troublemaker.

There is a whole lot more to the discipline record than what meets the eyes. Your discipline record also dictates what kind of academic student you are. Even though discipline problems are related to poor academics, some students make it to college with a very poor discipline record. Poor discipline records indicate a lot of time out of the classroom. You will spend time in the office waiting to see an administrator and listening to how you should act in school, or time in the guidance counselor's office answering questions about what is going on in your life that's making you behave badly, or time out of school or in In-School Suspension where there is no contact with peers. Attending classes are most important in college, even if you are taking virtual classes or an online class. There is always a way to check your attendance which is equivalent to being in a classroom.

From the moment you set foot on a college campus, you are on your own to make decisions based on the school code of conduct outlined in the student handbook. Read it. There is a code of conduct handbook at your school. Have you read it? Do you know what is expected of you while you are at school each day or what the consequences are for making a wrong decision? I advise you to read the handbook and to begin practicing now how to make sound decisions that will help you get ahead and maybe even help you foster stronger relationships with teachers and others at the school. We know that anyone can get into trouble or cause a problem, but bad discipline is closely associated with students who are average to below average academically. If you know, and most of us do, that you have a problem controlling your temper, then you might need to seek professional help.

College is a place where most students are in a transitional phase of life. Most people consider students as adults. Meanwhile most students act immaturely which makes it easier to hear or see something that could upset them. If not strong enough, a conversation could ignite a spark that could make you do or say something that you might regret for the rest of your life. What you say could surely cost you a friend or help you make an enemy.

Students who continuously act out in school are eventually written up by the teacher and sent to the principal's office. Students who act out at college are taken to the dean of their department. In high school, students are sent home for a few days, but in college, students are dismissed for the remainder of the semester. They may be unable to return. In high school, students lose a few days away from class which is not costly. In college, students lose the amount that it costs to be in school for the semester which could amount to as much as ten, fifteen, or thirty thousand dollars plus the time you need to repeat classes. Students who do not get their work done in high school, do not get to go to a top college. Students who do not get their work done in college, get to pay more to repeat classes, do not graduate on time or do not get a degree.

Build relationships with your teachers, administrators and other school personnel, as you will never know when or if you might need one of them to be a character reference for you. Show respect for yourself, peers, school and everyone. I loved high school, but I think I loved high school more after I graduated and realized that it was what I learned in high school that made it possible for me to succeed in college. My high school teachers did everything they could to open the windows of my mind to ensure I left knowing substantially more than before I came. I saw the future of a lot of my peers go down the drain because they lacked self-control and made a lot of bad decisions.

When I look back over the years, as you will also, I realized that everyone I attended high school with had the same opportunities that I did. You have the same opportunities as your peers, maybe more, but it is what you do with all of the opportunities that will make the difference in your life and everyone associated with you. One of the greatest moments in the life of human beings is one period of time they gain honor and respect. Success breeds respect. Get your act together and keep your act together at all times.

Another connotation for discipline denotes choosing an area of study that leads to a career of choice. Decide now what your discipline will be once you get to college. Work on it daily so you become an expert after college.

Chapter 10

GOAL SETTING

"If your mind can conceive it, you can achieve it." Setting goals is a miraculous way to plan what you are going to do. An insurance agent once told me that "we do not plan to fail; we fail to plan." Life is full of challenges. It is full of successful plans and some that failed. As people travel through life, sometimes planning successes does not phase adults. Fun and games are the way to go, but when reality sets in, usually after something major in life: death of a family member, foreclosure of the home, denial of a loan, or loss of a job, so does regret.

Take the time to sit with your parents and plan your college experience. Search for the right college/university, so you are comfortable with the professors, other students, and activities sponsored by the institution. According to the cost, plan how many years you can attend that college. Keep in mind that a four-year college has pre-set curriculum courses for each semester. Plan to get your academic work done if you do not want to repeat courses. Repeating courses can cause you to stay in school longer than the planned four years or could cause you to attend summer school. Either way, you will end up paying more to repeat courses.

Talk with your parents about who will be responsible for the expense of paying for college. Try to convince your parents that you do not want a college bill after graduation. Get a scholarship, or ask your parents to pay the college bill. Some parents start preparing for their child to go to college during the child's preschool years, and parents use those funds to cover the cost of their child's education. As long as the parents are willing to pay for the college education, the child should show gratitude by completing all academic commitments in a timely manner. On the other hand, some parents plan financially for their child to go to college, but sometimes unplanned events happen and those college funds have to be used. Then there is the parent who did not plan at all. Opps! Maybe the parent couldn't plan for college expenses due to fact that they are living from paycheck to paycheck. The burden of paying for college now rests on the child, if the child wants to go to college. Even if you attend a small private college, paying for four years of college could still cost as much as $100,000.00 when you include clothes, travel, pocket change, academic accessories, organizational dues, summer school, transportation, etc.

So here is what is unbelievable. There are children who make it to college and take courses for up to 5 years or more, including summer school, to complete a degree program. Summer school is an extra added expense. Students should attend summer school if graduating early is an option or making up a course or two in order to graduate within the four years period. Think about this! If you have to pay for your own college education, you will have debt when you graduate. Plan now to get a scholarship that pays for college. Find out what funds from your state will pay for your education and what the criteria is to quality for those funds. If you need a GPA of 3.0, then work hard to get it. Your hard work will pay off with the SAT and ACT scores.

If you are athletically talented, work hard to get an athletic scholarship. Some athletic scholarships pay for all expenses: books, tuition, room and board, and summer school. Try not to become an athlete who abuses the situation by getting a scholarship, then not completing course work, failing classes because of nonattendance and always changing majors to maintain eligibility to participate in sports. With a full ride to college, there is no way any athlete should graduate and not have an applicable degree. Athletes go wrong when they put more emphasis on playing the sport and not enough focus on academics. Time management is very important when in college and committed to an athletic scholarship.

If you are involved in extra-curricular activities when you get to college, you could qualify for the work-study program. You will have limited weekly hours to work, but you could get to help with a research project, the yearbook staff, ITT repairs, assistant in a department and more. The main thing is to stay focused on academics. Keep in mind that when you work a part-time job while taking classes, you decrease the number of hours that you could spend studying. Personally, I do not advise students to work a part-time or full time job while taking classes. Once you get behind in your course work, stress sets in, making it hard to concentrate and keep up with all of the work you will have to do for each class. Now you might say, "Oh, I'll get it done," and you might, but what will be the quality of the work?

Once at the college of your choice, a student advisor will be assigned to you. Develop a relationship with your advisor by planning regular visits to check the progress through your career program. Always know where you are in your degree program. You have four years to get in and successfully get out of school. There is space at the end of this chapter for you to write down your immediate short term goals and your long range goals. In five years from the day you write down your goals, check to see if you met your goals, are on target to meet the goals or just where you are in reference to meting your goals.

Take some time and complete the goal setting sheets in the next chapter. The sheets are designed for you to complete one set per year starting at the 8th grade year. If you start reading this book after your 8th grade year, you can complete the sheets based on what you remember about your thoughts given to planning for college.

GOAL SETTING

8th Grade Year

You may change your mind many times before you get to college, but make some decisions now. Make your decisions based on what is going on in your life now. Write down what's in your thinking right now. Research questions that you do not have answers for.

Right now, I would like _____ as a career for the rest of my life.

Three reasons why I chose this career are: _____
_____
_____
_____
_____

I chose this career because I was inspired by: _____
_____

The core subjects I need for a good background in this chosen career are: _____
_____

In case of an emergency in my life, for assistance/comfort I would see _____. I would see this person because: _____
_____
_____

If a bully approached me, the person I trust to talk with about the bully is _____ because _____
_____
_____

Adult persons whom I have a relationship at school or at home are
_____

_____

_____

The extra-curricular activities that I am involved in are _____

_____

_____

My favorite subjects are _____

_____

I feel I am or am not doing my best in school because: _____

_____

_____

_____

I believe my parents will/will not accept my career decision because

_____

_____

_____

_____

_____

_____

_____

_____

_____

_____

_____

_____

_____

_____

_____

_____

_____

_____

_____

_____

_____

GOAL SETTING

9th Grade Year

By now, you may have changed your mind about your chosen career. Continue on this page making the changes where necessary. Make your decisions based on what is going on in your life right now. Think carefully about your decisions because you are working now towards that career. If you are still interested in the career you chose last year, then just answer the necessary changes below.

I am not interested in _____ as a career for the rest of my life.

I am now interested in _____ as a career for the rest of my life.

Three reasons why I chose another career are: _____
_____
_____
_____

I chose this new career because I was inspired by: _____
_____
_____
_____

The core subjects I need for a good background in this new chosen career are: _____
_____
_____
_____

In case of an emergency in my life, for assistance/comfort I would talk with _____

I would see this person because: _____
_____

If a bully approached me, the person I trust to talk with about the
bully is _____ because he/she _____

_____

_____

Adult persons with whom I have a relationship at school/home are

_____

_____

_____

The extra-curricular activities that I am involved in are _____

_____

_____

My favorite subjects are _____

_____

I feel I am or am not doing my best in school because _____

_____

_____

_____

_____

I believe my parents will/will not accept my career decision because

_____

_____

_____

_____

_____

_____

_____

_____

_____

_____

_____

_____

Dr. Mable Scott

GOAL SETTING

10th Grade Year

By 10th grade, you should be narrowing your selection for a career and focusing on the courses you need to take in college with an acceptable GPA, ACT, and SAT Score. Continue on this page making the changes where necessary. Make your decisions based on what is going on in your life right now. Think carefully about your decisions because you are working now towards that career. If you are still interested in the career you chose last year, then just answer the necessary changes below.

I am not interested _____ as a career for the rest of my life.

I am now interested _____ as a career for the rest of my life.

Three reasons why I chose this career are: _____
_____
_____
_____

I chose this career because I was inspired by: _____
_____
_____
_____

The core subjects I need for a good background in this chosen career are: _____
_____
_____
_____

In case of an emergency in my life, for assistance/comfort I would see _____. I would see this person because: _____
_____

_____
_____
_____

If a bully approached me, the person I trust to talk with about the
bully is _____ because _____

_____
_____

Adult persons with whom I have a relationship at school/home are

_____
_____
_____

The extra-curricular activities that I am involved in are _____

_____
_____
_____

My favorite subjects are _____

_____
_____

I feel I am or am not doing my best in school because _____

_____
_____
_____
_____
_____
_____
_____
_____
_____
_____
_____
_____
_____
_____

GOAL SETTING

11th Grade Year

It is now time to look at a few colleges and universities. Most high school students want to know what to look for in a school of higher learning. Look for a school that offers the career that you are interested in. Talk with your parents about how your education will be funded. Take the SAT during this junior year of high school.

I have decided my career will be _____
_____
_____ for the rest of my life.

Three colleges/universities I am considering and have completed an application are:

Name   Location
_____
_____
_____

I chose these colleges/universities because _____
_____
_____
_____

I have successfully taken the core subjects below that are needed to graduate from high school and to be accepted in the college/university of my choice. _____
_____
_____
_____

The SAT score I need for admission to the college/university of my choice is _____ and the ACT score needed is _____. My current SAT score is _____ and my current ACT score is _____.

Adult persons who have encouraged me to go to college are: _____

_____

_____

_____

I feel I am or am not doing my best in school because _____

_____

_____

_____

To Do List (during the summer after your 10th grade.)

- ❑ Start taking college courses in high school that might fit your career choice.

- ❑ Job shadow someone who has a career that you want to pursue in college.

- ❑ Start a savings account. Learn to budget your money.

- ❑ Narrow decision for college/university of choice.

- ❑ Complete application online or obtain from school.

- ❑ Retake SAT/ACT if needed.

- ❑ If Grade Point Average (GPA) is 3.0 or better, check for state/school scholarships or start process for a loan.

- ❑ Secure transportation if allowed at school.

- ❑ Begin gathering needed academic tools.

- ❑ If you work, remember that college is first. Make work fit your schedule.

GOAL SETTING

12th Grade Year

By now, you should have narrowed down your list of colleges and universities to a first and second choice. You should know if the school provides everything that you are looking for and need to support your chosen career. You and your parents should have already decided how your higher education will be paid and the process started if a loan is needed. Take the SAT/ACT again if your score is not where you need it to be.

I have decided my career will be _____ for the rest of my life.

The college/university I have chosen and am seeking admission is to _____ Name Location

I chose this college/university because _____
_____
_____
_____

This college/university is _____ miles away from my home. This school allows freshmen to/not to have a car so my parents will/will not have provide me with transportation. I will live on campus. The name of my dormitory is _____. I have my room number and my roommate is _____.

My arrival date to campus is _____

I am very excited because _____
_____
_____
_____
_____

Dr. Mable Scott

APHORISMS TO REMEMBER

Below are some old sayings that my mom, grandmother, and teachers shared with me as I grew up. None of them created any of these aphorisms, but they used them to get their points across. If you can relate to half of these, I would say you are on your way to being successful. I did not research these aphorisms to identify the authors, and it is not my intention to take another's sayings, but these quotes brought me from a mighty long way, and they will help you as well.

Remember, the golden rule is "do unto others as you would have them do unto you."

If you think you can, then you can. On the other hand, if you think you can't, then you can't.

Whatever your mind can conceive, you can achieve.

Two heads are better than one. Seek help while in school.

Successful people do down board thinking before they make a move.

An empty wagon makes a lot of noise.

You are known by the company you keep.

Put God first, then your family, then career.

Love doesn't hurt.

There is no road that doesn't have an end.

If the heat is too hot, stay out of the kitchen.

If the shoe fits, wear it.

Beauty is in the eyes of the beholder.

Don't kick a man when he is down.

If it doesn't fit, don't force it.

If you do not have anything good to say about someone, don't say anything at all.

A friend in need is a friend indeed.

Friends don't let friends drive drunk.

It takes one to know one.

If it is to be, it is up to me.

If you mess with trash, it will blow in your eyes.

If you lay with the dogs, you will get fleas.

What goes around comes around.

What you do in the dark eventually comes to light.

What you speak about you bring about!!!

A man who does not read is no better off than the man who cannot see.

Live and let live.

It takes a friend to be a friend.

Oh, what a tangled web we weave, when first we venture to deceive.

If you talk the talk, be able to walk the walk.

It takes two to tango.

Choose or be chosen.

Play on the team or own the team.

Proper prior planning prevents pitiful poor performance.

REFERENCES

Brunstein, K. A., Marrocco, F., Kleinman, M., et. al. (2007). Bullying, depression, and suicidality in adolescents. *J A+ Acadlesc Psychiatry*. 46: 40-49.

Hodge, T. F. (2000). From Within I Rise: Spiritual Triumph Over Death and Conscious Encounter with "The Devine Prescience". Publish America.

Holy Bible, New International Version. (1973). Biblica, Inc.

Leigher, M. (2000). College Survival Skills. Clemson University

Lenz, B. (2007). What Does It Mean to Be College Ready? Helping All Students Get There. Teacher Leadership.

Marano, E. H., (2008). How to Poke Fun. Psychology Today.

Olweus, D. (1994) Bullying at school. Basic facts and an effective intervention program. Promote Education. Vol I (4): 27-31. 48.

Schwartz, J. (2010). Bullying, Suicide, Punishment. The New York Times.

Science Daily. (2009). No Bullies Here: Student Labels of 'Bullying' Can Be Misleading

Wikipedia. (2012).

www.ingramcontent.com/pod-product-compliance
Lightning Source LLC
Chambersburg PA
CBHW050402290526
45786CB00003B/1094